The Happily Ever After Handbook

The Happily Ever After Handbook

52 Things You Can Do to Freshen Up Your Marriage

Daniel M. Klein

Andrews McMeel Publishing
Kansas City

 For information, write Andrews McMeel Publishing, an Andrews McMeel Universal company, 4520 Main Street, Kansas City, Missouri 64111.

www.andrewsmcmeel.com

99 00 01 02 03 RDC 10 9 8 7 6 5 4 3 2 1

Library of Congress Cataloging-in-Publication Data
Klein, Daniel M.
The happily ever after handbook : 52 things you can do to freshen up your marriage/Daniel M. Klein.
p. cm.
ISBN 0-8362-7866-6 (hd)
1. Marriage—United States—Psychological aspects. 2. Behavior modificaion—United States. 3. Attitude change—United States.
I. Title
HQ734.K617 1999
646.7'8—DC21 98-27881
CIP

To my wife, Freke, who has shown me that happiness transcends understanding

Contents

Contents

Introduction

Let's face it, weddings are easy.

It's happily ever after that's hard.

Because the minute the wedding ceremony is over and the happy couple is toasted, a time bomb is triggered. That time bomb is made up of a bundle of dynamite sticks called Lost Passion, Built-Up Anger, Boring Habits, Claustrophobia, and probably the most devastating of them all, Deadly Seriousness.

Of course, there are the traditional methods for avoiding these hazards. Going into total denial has been known to work quite well. Prayer has proven effective in a few isolated cases. And, of course, there is couple's therapy, which gives you the opportunity to talk over your complaints and disappointments and recriminations ad nauseam at $100-plus per session for years, even decades.

Or you can try the fifty-two things I've put together here. Not only are they a bargain, but if you give them a real chance, you actually can renew, refresh, and reimpassion your marriage.

These fifty-two interpersonal adventures and psychological exercises probably are not what you'd expect from a long-time student of psychology. But I've never put much stock in simply talking out conflicts between partners—because it turns out that the actual content of our arguments is pretty irrelevant in the long run. Marital anger has a life of its own separate from actual issues. So the best way to deal with it is by doing things like scheduling nonverbal screamfests or crowding out hostile feelings with playful fun and games. In other words, I don't believe marital relationships can be negotiated, but they sure as hell can be invigorated.

Introduction

What we've got here are not only fifty-two ways to freshen up your marriage, but fifty-two ways to make it warm and funny and unpredictable and sexy all over again.

Take it seriously—but, please, not too seriously!

2.

Admit to Weaknesses, Even If You Have to Make Them Up

She says, "Why don't you send your steak back, since you think it's overdone?"

Your instinct is to retort, "Hey, it's my steak! I'll do what I want with it, okay?"

But instead you say, "I know I should. But it just makes me feel so damned uncomfortable doing that kind of thing."

Now, what did you lose by saying that? Some pride, right? You experienced a brief moment of wimpiness. But who cares? Because what you have gained is a pleasant, unruffled evening out with your wife.

—

He says, "Doesn't that skirt look a little too, you know, *girlish* for you?"

Your instinct is to come back with, "You don't exactly look like Brad Pitt in those jeans yourself!"

But instead you say, "I know, hon, but I just felt kind of young and festive tonight, so I thought I'd wear it anyhow."

Again, what was lost—a little pride? Who cares? The night is young!

Remember: Pride is a glut on the emotional market. But happiness, especially marital happiness, is a rare and precious commodity.

I

The Five Basic Principles of a Happy Marriage

1.

Never Go to Sleep Angry at Each Other

Anger grows in your sleep—that's a biological fact. By the time you wake up in the morning there is a six-headed monster doing calisthenics in your stomach. This little guy builds a steel cage around your heart, poisons your words, and gives you gas.

Obviously, not every disagreement can be resolved before bedtime. And who wants to stay up all night talking out your basic differences in exquisite psychological detail—*yet again?* Instead, try one or two or three of the exercises under **Five Exercises to Reduce Messy Anger Buildup.** At the very least, you will go to sleep exhausted, and that in itself can dissipate much of the anger.

3.

Always Keep Your Eye on the Big Picture, Even If the Frustration of the Moment Puts Murderous Thoughts in Your Head

You put your key in the ignition and discover that he left you without any gas in the tank.

The thought of shoving him off the top of a twenty-story building flashes unbidden through your mind.

So you walk back into your house, brew a fresh cup of coffee, and read the front page of the newspaper. You read about wars and civil strife all over the globe, refugees, starvation, misery. After ten minutes of this, you phone the garage and ask them to send over a canister of gasoline.

This is not to say that you don't let your mate know what a thoughtless s.o.b. he was when you talk to him later. But you've kept it in perspective, and that makes for a long, happy marriage.

4.

Say "Please" and "Thank You" to Each Other

I know what you are thinking: This is starting to sound like Mister Rogers.

But it turns out that old-time polite behavior is one of the surest ways of ensuring a long and satisfying relationship.

"Thanks for the coffee," "Please pass the salt," and even "What a nice dinner—thanks a lot, hon," keep the edges of a marriage from getting brittle.

Sure, it's corny and retro and formal. But formality is just what a good marriage needs—a bit of distance and deference makes those intimate moments all the more intimate.

5.

Try to Make Love Whenever Your Partner Wants to—Even If You Are Not Particularly in the Mood

For one thing, once you push yourself to do it, nine times out of ten you'll find that you actually get into the mood. And then you'll be glad you did.

For another thing, if you keep waiting for that perfect moment when both of you are in the mood at exactly the same time, you'll probably discover that you are only making love every other month. By making sex into such a big deal, you can end up "pricing" it out of your daily budget. And a marriage without regular lovemaking very quickly drifts into boredom and testiness.

Obviously, I'm not talking about giving in to sexual coercion of any kind. And, of course, if one partner is always the one who initiates lovemaking and the other is always the Goer-Along, resentments can build. But the best response for all Goers-Along is to start taking the initiative yourself once in a while. That will be sexually energizing for both of you.

II

Five Adventures to Renew Your Consciousness of Each Other

6.

Strangers in a Strange Town

It's a Saturday and you've both left the weekend free of work and social obligations. You take out a map of your state and put it on the floor. Then you stick a thumbtack on your town and attach a thread that extends one hundred "map" miles. One of you dons a blindfold, swings the thread around and around, and stops. Where you stop is your destination for the day.

You pack a light overnight bag and drive to your mystery destination (or better yet, take a train or bus there). Once you arrive, you start walking. *You are strangers in a strange town.* You have no idea where you are going to sleep, where you are going to eat, what you are going to find here. You have only each other for company. You have only each other to rely on.

That's it. The rest takes care of itself. Because as the day and night progresses, you will gradually find yourselves experiencing each other in ways you have probably forgotten—your vulnerabilities, your resources, your mutual dependencies, your sense of adventure.

You will return home Sunday afternoon with a renewed awareness of one another. And a special bond.

7.

Marathon Tearjerker Evening

Together, go to the video rental shop and pick up at least three of your all-time favorite sentimental movies. We're talking three-hanky movies like *The Way We Were* and *Bambi* and *The Bridges of Madison County.*

Now make a light supper with lots of wine and turn on the answering machine. Then sit down together in front of the TV for a Marathon Tearjerker Evening. Let go and cry your loving eyes out.

It is a little-known fact that crying together is as intimate an experience as coming together. (Not only that, but the one often leads to the other.)

8.

Picking Up Where You Left Off

Select a bar or diner where you are extremely unlikely to run into anyone either of you know. (A hotel bar is often good for this adventure.)

Leaving your home separately one half hour apart, go to this bar, and pretend that you do not know each other. Staying in the role of strangers will not be easy (you'll tend to giggle a lot at first), but stick with it—it's worth it.

Now, *pick each other up . . . very, very slowly.*

Flirt with each other like crazy. Gradually get to know one another.

Then, if you get lucky, take each other home.

9.

Dearest Beloved

The next time either of you goes away on a business trip for more than three nights, make a promise *not* to phone each other (except for genuine emergencies).

Instead, fax letters to each other daily—or more than daily if time permits. (Most hotels have fax facilities and most neighborhoods have places such as copy shops and office-supply stores for sending and receiving faxes.) You will find that you communicate things to one another that you would not say on the phone (or face to face, for that matter). Personal things. Poetic things. Things that flow more easily from the hand than from the mouth.

What you will be doing is re-creating the days

when long-distance calls were expensive and loving couples wrote letters when they were separated. There is something special about these letters: You can linger over them. Reread them. And you can save them and read them again at times when you need help remembering why you got married to this person.

10.

River Wild

Go white-water rafting together.

Think you're too old? Think it's too dangerous?

Good. Do it anyway. (It's not really that dangerous.)

Being in a situation of peril together suddenly makes you more alert to each other in ways you may have forgotten—or never even knew. Instead of your perennial Planning-the-Future/Chewing-Over-the-Past Selves interacting, your Spontaneous, Heightened-Senses, In-the-Moment Selves meet and touch.

"Watch out!" "Dig to the left!" "Wow! Beautiful!"

It's enough to make you fall in love all over again.

III

Five Exercises to Reduce Messy Anger Buildup

11.

High Decibel, Low Impact (Nonverbal)

Turn on your CD player up to top volume and play something relentlessly feverish, like *Carmina Burana* or the Stones' *Sticky Fingers* album or something fetching by Twisted Sister.

Now together go down into the basement (if you live in an apartment, the bathroom will do), face each other at a distance of no less than five feet, and *scream bloody murder at each other for fifteen straight minutes!* (Have a clock in full view.)

No real words are allowed. Just inchoate, raw screaming.

When your time is up, stop immediately. Then come right back upstairs and go about your business as if nothing happened—make dinner, make love, go to the office, watch TV.

Schedule these sessions once a month, minimum. Messy anger buildup has to be relieved on a regular basis even if you have been getting along famously. You'll be surprised by the radically reduced number of fights you'll have if you keep to this schedule. This exercise demonstrates how irrelevant the so-called content of your arguments usually is—how most of your arguments are simply the result of floating irritation. (Incidentally, you'll also be surprised at how often you'll want to make love after your screamfests.)

12.

Theater of the Absurd

Spend one half hour pretending you are another couple—a couple who don't get along at all. Choose from among your friends (this shouldn't be hard) or from public figures (Roseanne and Whoever She's Currently Married To is always a good option).

Now have a "proxy" marital fight. Be sure to call each other by your "role" names only. Be sure to fight about issues in *their* lives, not yours (although some overlap is inevitable). Fight dirty. Call each other nasty names.

This exercise can reduce anger buildup more effectively than any other, but it has been known on occasion to get a bit dicey. If tempers grow too hot and you forget it's just a game, stop on the spot and go back to Exercise 11.

13.

Pajama Party

Gather all the pillows in the house, get into your jammies, stand on either side of your bed, and have a pillow fight.

Stop at exhaustion.

If both of you are up for it, continue on the bed with a tickle fight. (Post-tickling sex is optional.)

14.

High Decibel, More Impact (Verbal)

As in Exercise 11, turn up your CD player, go down into the basement (or into the bathroom), stand at five feet, and scream at each other like crazy for fifteen full minutes.

This time, however, *real names* and *real words* are allowed.

But what is *not* allowed are *real issues!*

In other words, go ahead and scream, "You're a real bastard, Ted!" or "What a bitch you are, Edith! Were you born that way or did it take years of practice?"

That's just fine and dandy.

But what is *not* permitted is, "How could you humiliate me like that in front of my sister?" or "If you think he's so damned attractive, why don't you have an affair with him!"

These are not allowed because this is the normal stuff of marital fights and is guaranteed to get you nowhere except more angry. Remember, the content of your gripes and recriminations with each other is usually overrated—anger has a life of its own.

Warning: This exercise has been know to get scary. It should be used only when anger has been building up for so long that it's about to burst out one way or another anyhow.

15.

Voodoo Too?

Make an effigy doll of your mate and keep it in your sock drawer.

At those moments when the urge to mutilate and kill your mate arises (in the average marriage, roughly once a week), take out the effigy and pound on its head. Stick pins in it. Rub dirt on it. Twist its arm. Curse at it. Then stick it back in your sock drawer.

Sound ridiculous?

You bet.

But consider this: The divorce rate among practitioners of voodoo is roughly 10 percent that of the rest of us. How crazy can they be? *(Okay, I made that up—but I bet I'm right.)*

IV

Five Imaginary Plots for Facing the Alternative

16.

There-but-for-the-Grace-of-God-Go-I Weekend

Spend a weekend with a recently divorced, same-sex friend.

Wallow in your friend's newfound freedom.

But then gradually tune in to the dailiness of his or her life: the going out on blind dates again, the only seeing your own children at appointed times, the eating sesame noodles alone in front of the TV three nights in a row.

By Sunday evening, eating sesame noodles with your mate starts to look good, doesn't it?

17.

Can This Marriage Be Saved?

Help friends who are having marital problems sort things out. Together, make a real project of it, doing the very best job that you can.

Talk to this couple separately, talk to them together. Help them see each other's point of view on the issues that divide them. Help them find compromises and common ground. Promise to be there for them when things between them get tough again.

That's the whole deal.

Miraculously, you will have done more to ensure the happiness of your *own* marriage than you could have imagined.

18.

Making Whoopee

There is a person at work about whom you have wild sexual fantasies. (Don't ask how I know this—I have my sources.)

Now, without your fully realizing it, these fantasies make you feel just the slightest bit dissatisfied with your mate when you get home. The Old Spouse just doesn't seem as exciting or erotic after these imaginary wild encounters with Person X in a stalled elevator.

Well, instead of stopping these fantasies, expand on them. That's right, take them the whole route: After doing the nasty in the elevator, imagine leaving your partner so you can spend *all* of your time with Person X. Fantasize about washing the dishes with him or her; fantasize about waiting for Person X to get out of the bathroom already—you're late for work. Fantasize about picking up Person X's socks.

And here's the bubble-breaker: Imagine your relationship ten years from now!

Now honestly, was it worth that quickie in the elevator?

19.

Reading the Impersonals

Buy copies of magazines with extensive personal ads in them. Be sure to select magazines that correspond to your general social type.

Sit down alone at the kitchen table and go through the ads, imagining that you really are searching for a mate at this point in your life.

"**DWF, 40ish,** brainy, beautiful, playful Brahms 4th type, seeks SWM financially secure, ethical vegetarian for long walks by the sea."

"**Effervescent SWM,** balding but fit nonsmoker, seeks witty, fun-loving, financially secure SWF for long walks in the mountains."

If reading a half dozen of these doesn't send you scurrying from the room in a panic and begging your mate to forgive you for whatever wrongs you may have committed in the past ten years, then try sitting down and composing your *own* personal ad. Somehow it all makes that semibrainy, semibeautiful, Brahms-shmahms type you have been living with seem like the person of your dreams, doesn't it?

20.

The Reason Y

Spend a weekend alone in a single-occupancy hotel or at the YMCA or YWCA.

Have breakfast alone in the local coffee shop.

Have lunch alone in the local coffee shop.

Have dinner alone in the local Chinese restaurant.

Watch the Celtics get walloped in the local sports bar.

Go to bed alone.

If you don't return home Sunday night with a desire to renew your marital vows, then no man ever loved, nor this man ever writ.

V

Five Good Sports to Rebuild Your Mutual Trust

21.

Seeing-Eye Lover

Take turns pretending that you are blind. (Those little black plastic doodads you wear under the tanning machine do the trick nicely—and they can be covered with dark glasses.)

Now go out for a long walk around town, the "seeing" partner leading the "blind" one. Take this exercise seriously—get the feel of your total dependence on your Seeing-Eye Lover, what it means for you emotionally to put all your trust in him or her.

Think about why you hate that feeling.

Think about why you love it.

Now switch.

22.

Is There a Doctor in the House?

The next time one of you comes down with a cold or the flu, let your partner take total care of you.

"Get right into bed!" he or she barks, sounding very much like your mother, and you dutifully scramble under the covers.

Soon it's time to have your temperature taken, then time to take your medicine, then time to pull down the shades and nap for an hour—no TV! Get the picture?

But then it's time for your alcohol rub and hot compresses and mustard plaster. ("Mustard plaster?" Don't question the doctor!)

Feel yourself surrendering to your partner's ministrations.

Feel yourself getting better.

23.

Hop-Along Capacity

Remember those three-legged races at the Memorial Day picnic?

Here's the way they go: One person ties their right ankle to the other person's left ankle (a bandana is traditionally used). Now in order to walk around, the two of you have to coordinate your mutual "middle" leg.

Try doing this during the half hour after dinner when there are chores to be done: putting out the trash, washing the dishes, folding the laundry.

This one turns out to be not only an exercise in trust and cooperation, but an exercise in learning to appreciate your separateness—the joys of your own space.

Extra credit: Take a three-legged shower together.

24.

Unsplintering Your Relationship

The next time you get a splinter, ask your partner to remove it for you. Once your partner appears at your side with straight pin and tweezers in hand, you are not allowed to say a word!

Not "Isn't that pin too big?"

Not "For god's sake, be careful!"

Not "Shouldn't you put on your reading glasses?"

"Ouch!" is permitted, but only two of those.

Trust your partner!

25.

Unmentionables

Volunteer to go to the store and purchase something for your partner that makes you feel very uncomfortable or embarrassed.

If you are a man, Tampax fills the bill nicely.

If you are a woman, a jock strap should do the trick.

Do it like a grown-up. No long-winded explanations to the sales clerk permitted. No smirking either.

Do a good, trustworthy job.

There, that wasn't so hard, was it?

VI

Five Games to Make Your Marriage More Playful (and Less Deadly Serious)

26.

Naked Dinner

On an evening when there's no one home but the two of you, pull down the shades and get naked. Then cook and eat dinner together.

Messy food is highly recommended. We're talking cheese fondue, fettuccine Alfredo, sour-cream dips, and peach cobbler.

Feed each other. Drip a little Alfredo sauce on your shoulder and let your partner lick it off. Take it from there. Be imaginative.

Feel silly? Childish? Stupid?

Terrific! That means you're doing it right.

It probably also means that you've been acting too "grown-up" and serious with each other for too damned long.

27.

Stark and Seek

While you're still starkers, play a game of hide-and-seek.

Yell "Warmer!" when your Seeker gets close.

Yell whatever you please when he or she finds you.

28.

Cat's Away

Pretend you are still living at home with your parents. Now pretend that they are going away for the weekend.

Invite your "boyfriend" (husband) or "girlfriend" (wife) over for a sneaky party for two.

Buy a case of beer. Get out your old Elvis records. Your Little Richard records. And (depending on how old you are) your Frank Sinatra records.

Dance cheek-to-cheek in the rec room. Make out. Talk about how uptight your parents are. Make out. Talk about how you're going to be different from your parents when you grow up (and if you are doing the exercises in this book, you are).

Make out.

29.

Twist and Shout!

Stock up on games that you both used to love before you decided that your life was too serious and busy for play: Ping-Pong, Monopoly, tiddledywinks, Twister. (Remember Twister? Well, there's still a copy in your downstairs closet somewhere.)

Set aside a half hour after dinner once a week.

Now forget everything else that happened that day, let go of whatever agenda you have going with each other, and Play!

No excuses. It's only a half hour. And it will do more to lighten up your mutual emotional burden than a $100 session of couples therapy. (This is a well-documented fact that the American Psychological Association is trying desperately to hide from you.)

30.

Play It Again, Sam

Find someone who plays the piano. Find a piano (portable) and put it in your living room for the night.

Throw a Sing-Along Party.

Invite only folks who know how to have fun. (No one who makes fun of having fun permitted.)

Hand out song sheets at the door (maybe a nice mix of oldies, show tunes, Beatles, Donovan, and Dylan) and go directly to the piano. No cocktail banter, no posturing, no political discussions. Just sing your loving hearts out!

Sing until you drop.

Now, didn't that feel good? It's kind of fun being a fun couple, isn't it?

VII

Five Ways to Rekindle Sexual Excitement in Your Marriage

31.

Getting to the Root of Sensuality

Give each other shampoos. Long, gentle, sudsy shampoos with warm water. The Shampooee may sit in a chair by the sink or in a bathtub.

Rinse and wash again.

Sounds pretty tame, doesn't it?

But the fact is that hand-to-head contact is probably the most intimate, tender, love-inducing physical contact there is. No, I didn't say the most erotic. But somehow, once that tender, loving hand-to-head contact is made, the sexy stuff follows quite naturally.

32.

Hello? Can You Feel Me?

In the middle of the morning close your office door, call up your mate, and talk dirty.

Describe in luscious sensual detail the unspeakable things you imagine doing to her or him. Hold nothing back. Moan, groan, breathe hard.

If it makes it less embarrassing, *schedule* your first phone-sex encounter. And maybe your second. But the third time should be a spontaneous surprise.

Optional: Rush out to meet each other at a motel room in the middle of the phone call.

33.

Steamy Weekend

Make weekend reservations at one of those hotels that has heart-shaped tubs and vibrating beds.

Right, I know it's terribly corny and déclassé. But it may also be just the thing your all-too-predictable marriage needs to become romantic and erotic again.

Go the whole route. Drink champagne in bed. Order up oysters from room service. Watch *Emmanuelle* on the pay-per-view TV.

And don't worry about what your friends think. You can always tell them you went on a meditation retreat at the Kripalu Institute.

34.

"Lower, Andre. Lower."

Buy a massage table and put it in your bedroom. Buy scented massage oil.

Take turns giving each other massages.

Real massages, none of those two-minute shoulder rubs that you've been passing off as the genuine article all these years. One half-hour minimum apiece.

The Massagee is encouraged to give specific directions to the Massager. Like "Lower, Andre" or "Harder, Gretchen."

Try to schedule these sessions on a regular basis; at the very least, don't let a month go by without one double massage session.

And here's the rub: Never interrupt a massage

to skip directly to making love. (I'm not being perverse—I guarantee that you'll both enjoy the lovemaking all the more if you knead your way up to it.)

35.

I've Got a Secret

Sit on opposite sides of a dimly lit room facing each other. Now alternate telling each other your secret sexual fantasies.

Describe your fantasies exactly the way you imagine them. Don't hurry and don't skimp on the details. Be as honest and revealing as you can without making yourself or your partner jealous. (For example, keep the phantom lovers in your scenarios nameless.) Close your eyes if it makes either the Telling or the Listening easier.

Postconfessional lovemaking is optional. It is also probable.

VIII

Five Ways to Change Marital Habits

36.

Smooth Move

Move out of your old bedroom into a new one—say, into the guest room or maybe switch bedrooms with one of your kids.

Now, starting from scratch, create a bedroom that you both love.

A new bed or maybe even separate beds. (Separate beds have been much maligned—often as not they make for *more* sex in your lives!) A new rug. New pictures on the walls. New closet arrangements.

Sounds like a lot of trouble, doesn't it?

Well, the fact is that when you change bedrooms, you automatically change the ways you relate to each other in the bedroom. And after ten or so years together, that is invariably for the better.

37.

Not the Same Old Same Old

Throw a dinner party for the people you really find interesting instead of for the people you feel obligated to have over.

Draw up your invitation lists separately.

Invite that new kid in the mail room, the one who is always telling jokes. And that woman you met in the elevator who used to live in Thailand. And that old high school friend who you've been meaning to call all these years.

Invite everybody on both of your lists. Don't worry about whether or not it's a good mix.

Make a fabulous dinner.

Not only will you have a wonderful evening, you will discover parts of yourself and each other that have been deeply buried under social habits for years.

38.

Can I Borrow Your Notes?

Take lessons in something together. Not the obvious stuff like ballroom dancing or French—those can raise the usual conflicts, like arguments about who's leading or who's in a position to correct the other's accent.

But how about flamenco lessons? No questions about who's leading here. No problems of role definition. Just an exotic body-trip together.

Or how about bungee-jumping lessons or aikido or something truly weird like a course in fingerprinting?

Carry her books home.

Do your homework together.

39.

Making Up

Schedule an entire day for both of you at a unisex beauty spa.

Get the whole works: the sauna, the massage, the pedicure.

Then, after consulting with the beautician together, get a makeover—each of you.

Go for a totally new look. Maybe something French. Maybe something retro. Maybe something terribly young.

Now, why is it that you both feel like making love the minute you leave?

40.

The Nick of Time

For an entire evening (or longer, if you like) call each other by new names. Make up your own new moniker.

Haven't you always wondered what it would be like to be a Dolores?

Or a Lance?

Didn't you secretly envy that kid who answered to "Rebel"? Or the one everyone called "Bubbles"?

It's just a silly game, of course. But did you notice that sexy glint that came into his eye when you called him Lance?

IX

Five Gifts That Bind

41.

Surprise Package

Give your partner little presents for no reason whatsoever. Say, a pack of bubblegum with '50s movie-star trading cards. Or a cassette of old Greek folk songs. Or a canister of mango herbal tea.

Give it after dinner on a Tuesday evening. Or when you go to bed on Sunday night. This has nothing to do with birthdays or Christmas or job promotions—it is a surprise package, pure and simple.

For the truth is, a surprise pack of bubblegum on a Tuesday evening can be a more joyful and heartwarming gift than a cashmere sweater on Christmas.

42.

Le Mot Juste

Buy your mate a book of poetry. But not *any* book of poetry will do; not even any well-known or highly touted book of poetry will do. It has to be a book of poems that speak personally to your mate, that refer to ideas, images, feelings, and places that resonate for that person.

Mark the pages that contain the innermost secret meanings that you share with one another. Before presenting the book, read one of these special poems aloud to him or her.

43.

Twofer

Surprise your partner with a gift that is for the two of you. Say, a massage table that you both will use as you alternate giving each other massages. Or a bottle of that expensive, extra-virgin olive oil that you both admired so much at a friend's house. Or that ultimate twofer gift, a bicycle built for two.

Address the gift card to both of you.

44.

A Gift for the Inner (Possibly Naughty) Child

Buy your partner something that you know he or she really wants but, for any number of reasons, would be too embarrassed to buy for him or herself.

Do you think in his heart of hearts, he would really like a subscription to *Playboy*? What the hell—get it for him.

Do you think in her heart of hearts, she would really like a subscription to *Playgirl*? Make her happy.

If he wasn't so afraid of seeming like a case of arrested development, do you think he really would get a kick out of having some toy battleships to play with in the bathtub? Buy him some.

If she wasn't so afraid of seeming like her mother,

do you think she really would enjoy having a Mixmaster? Buy her one—she can always blame it on you.

45.

The Ultimate Sacrifice

Give your partner a gift that she or he really wants, but that you don't want—I mean, you *really* don't want it!

Say she adores opera and you would rather sleep on nails than sit through *La Traviata*. Okay, buy season's tickets to the opera *for both of you*.

Now that's a *real* gift!

Say he yearns for a La-Z-Boy in the middle of the living room and you would rather live in a basement apartment than have Naugahyde anywhere in your house. So what you do is you buy him a La-Z-Boy in moss-green Naugahyde for his very own.

These are the gifts that love is made of.

X

Five Memory Refreshers to Remind You Why You Married Each Other in the First Place

46.

Sentimental Journey

Take a weekend trip to the place where you first met.

Visit as many of the sites and do as many of the things that you did together at that time:

Catch a matinee at the Elgin (if it's still there), have breakfast at the 3 Brothers (if it's still there), make out in the car up near the reservoir, stay in that motel (you know the one).

Re-create the feel of that wonderfully romantic period as best you can.

And try to remember.

47.

Silent Night

Spend an entire evening together not talking. Zilch! Not even "Pass the salt."

Mysterious things will happen:

You will find yourselves looking at each other in new ways—without the fog of words to blur your vision.

You will suddenly find yourselves bursting into laughter.

You will find yourselves touching each other a whole lot more.

You will find yourselves remembering long-forgotten funny little reasons why you like each other.

Handwritten notes are permitted only for emergencies—for instance, "Your tie is on fire!"

48.

The Best of Times

Invite over the couple who are your oldest and best friends.

After dinner, start telling stories about the good old days of your relationship—how you met, your courtship, your best vacation, when your first child was born.

Just get the ball rolling. Soon your friends will be telling similar stories.

Keep it going.

Drink champagne.

Try and remember, and when you remember, let your heart follow.

49.

Photo Op

Get out that shoe box with all those old photographs in it.

Now get down on the living-room rug with a bottle of wine and go through them together.

That's it. Don't try to sort the photos in any particular order. Comment on them if you like, but don't if you don't feel like it.

Why are you both smiling so much?

50.

Groundhog Day

Sitting cozily together on the sofa (preferably in front of a blazing fire in the fireplace), discuss this question: "If we had to relive one day of our marriage over and over again eternally, what day would that be?"

Choose one (you can always choose a different one on another night). Together, reconstruct this day in as much detail as you can remember. Try to go hour by hour, feeling by feeling, for example, "You put on my favorites—your plaid boxers," "We burst out laughing every time the Tour Guide said, 'Walk this way,'" and "I caught you looking at me in the bathroom mirror." How would it feel if each time you relived this day you got deeper and deeper into it—closer and closer to what it is you love about that day? In that feeling is the essence of your marriage.

XI
One Modest Proposal

51.

A Modest Proposal

Propose to each other all over again.

Hey, you remembered!

XII
One Ceremony

52.

I Do . . . Again

Throw yourselves a wedding to end all weddings.

Invite only people you really want to be there (as compared to the first time around, when you invited people your *mother* really wanted to be there). Invite only people who believe in the beauty and sanctity of marriage (your cynical friends are permitted to come only to the reception).

Make the service as conventional or unconventional as you want. When you design your vows to one another, say only what you mean. When you declare your vows to one another, mean what you say.

Remember this moment forever.

DANIEL M. KLEIN is co-inventor of the original Group Therapy Game. A graduate of Harvard, he has ghostwritten many popular books on psychology, including *Tales from a Traveling Couch* and the best-seller *How to Make Love to the Same Person for the Rest of Your Life.* Klein has been happily married to the same woman for twenty-one years and still counting.